ACROSS FIVE APRILS

by
Irene Hunt

Teacher Guide

Written by
Anne Troy

Note

The Berkley/Pacer paperback edition of the book published by arrangement with Follett Publishing Company was used to prepare this guide. The page references may differ in the hardcover or other paperback editions.

Please note: Please assess the appropriateness of this book for the age level and maturity of your students prior to reading and discussing it with your class.

ISBN 1-56137-091-6

Copyright 2000 by Novel Units, Inc., San Antonio, Texas. All rights reserved. No part of this publication may be reproduced, stored in a retrieval system, or transmitted in any way or by any means (electronic, mechanical, photocopying, recording, or otherwise) without prior written permission from Novel Units, Inc., with the following exceptions: Photocopying of student worksheets by a teacher who purchased this publication for his/her own class is permissible. Reproduction of any part of this publication for an entire school or for a school system or for commercial sale is strictly prohibited. **Copyright infringement is a violation of Federal Law.**

Novel Units is a registered trademark of Novel Units, Inc.

Printed in the United States of America.

To order, contact your local school supply store, or—

Novel Units, Inc.
P.O. Box 791610
San Antonio, TX 78279

Web site: www.educyberstor.com

Table of Contents

Skills and Strategies

Thinking
    Brainstorming, classifying
    and categorizing, comparing
    and contrasting, evaluating,
    analyzing details

Comprehension
    Predicting, sequencing,
    cause/effect, inference,
    story mapping

Writing
    Response journal, chapter
    titles, diary

Vocabulary
    Word maps, antonym/
    synonym, context

Listening/Speaking
    Participation in discussion,
    participation in dramatic
    activities

Literary Elements
    Character, setting, plot
    development, point of view,
    conflict, tone, figurative
    language, dialect

Summary of *Across Five Aprils*

Across Five Aprils is a memorable story of the tragic years of the Civil War as experienced by a boy, his family, and neighbors in a backwoods community in southern Illinois. Through conversation and experience, the issues in the war gradually become clearer to Jethro. The main theme of the book is the effect of outside events upon a child growing up. One of Jethro's brothers joins the Confederate side and the others fight for the Union. Some members of the community turn against the family because they have a son fighting on the Confederate side. The family barn is burned and the well water filled with oil. The story emphasizes the futility of aggression. The details of battles and campaigns are integrated into letters and conversations. The author paints a believable young boy whose adolescence coincides with the period of the American Civil War.

About the Author

Irene Hunt was born and raised in Illinois. She attended the University of Illinois, A.B. 1939 and the University of Minnesota, M.A. 1946. She taught French and English, 1930-1945 in the Oak Park, Illinois public schools. Between 1946 and 1950, she taught at the University of South Dakota. Ms. Hunt returned to Illinois to act as a teacher and consultant in the Cicero, Illinois public schools.

Irene Hunt received the Charles W. Follett Award in 1964, the American Notable Book Award in 1965, and was the sole runner-up for the Newbery Medal, 1965, for *Across Five Aprils*. In 1967, she received the Newbery Medal for *Up a Road Slowly*.

Other Books by Irene Hunt

The Everlasting Hills; No Promises in the Wind; The Lottery Rose; Up a Road Slowly

Instructions Prior to Reading

You may wish to choose one or more of the following Prereading Discussion Questions and Activities. Each is designed to help students draw from their store of background knowledge about the events and themes they will meet in the story they are about to read.

Prereading Discussion Questions and Activities

1. **Previewing**
    Have the students examine the title and cover illustration. Also suggest that they look at the back cover. What do you think the story will be about? What do you think the title, *Across Five Aprils*, means?

2. **Map**
    Post a large map of the United States with Union and Confederate States marked by appropriate colors. (A small map is included on page 10 of this guide.)

© Novel Units, Inc.

All rights reserved

3. Concept Map

Write "Civil War" at the center of a large piece of paper. Brainstorm. Have students generate any ideas that come to mind when they hear the term, helping students organize them into categories such as: President, famous soldiers; time of the war; famous people in the Civil War, causes, effects, etc. Draw "wagon spokes" around the central concept to connect with the supporting ideas. Encourage students to add to the chart during and after their reading of the novel.

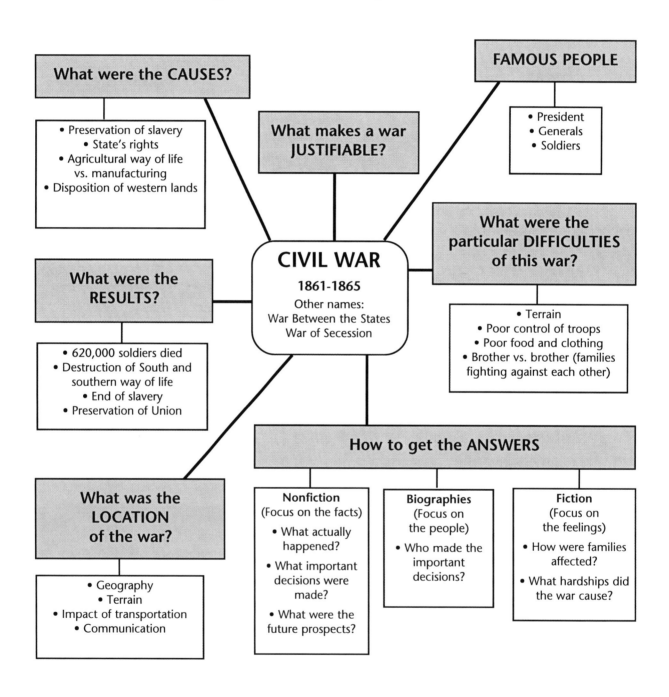

© Novel Units, Inc.

4

All rights reserved

4. Bulletin Boards

a) Find pictures of the dress of women and men in the 19th century. Compare the dress of soldiers in the Civil War and modern day soldiers.

b) Develop a comparison chart for the North and South at the time of the Civil War.

	NORTH	SOUTH
Economy	Mixed including agrarian and manufacturing	Agrarian
Ideals	Puritan ethic Individualism	Paternal Plantation System
Ways of Life	Individual effort Developing small businesses	Plantation Agricultural economy based on slave labor
Geography	Cooler climate Rocky soil Favored growth of cities	Warm climate Fertile soil
Population	22 million	9 million
Ideas on State's Rights	Favored primacy of federal rule	Favored state's rights
Flag		
Politics	New Republican Party emerged	New country formed

All rights reserved

5. Response Journal

The students will keep a response journal. The students will divide their papers in half (vertically). On the left side, they will write short summaries of what has happened in each section using their own words. On the right side, they will react to what they have read. Reactions include answers to such questions as: How would I have felt in the character's place? What is my opinion of what the character did? How did the character's situation remind me of my own life?

6. Time Line

Make a time line. Put each chapter and the major actions on the time line. (See page 9 of this guide.)

7. Anticipation Guide

Use the following Anticipation Guide. (See page 11 of this guide.)

Recommended Procedure

Teachers are encouraged to adapt this guide to meet the needs of individual classes and students. You know your students best. We are offering you some tools for working with them. Here are some of the nuts and bolts for using these "tools"— a glossary of some of the terms used that will facilitate your use of this guide.

Bloom's Taxonomy

A classification system for various levels of thinking. Questions keyed to these levels may be:
- Comprehension questions, which ask one to state the meaning of what is written;
- Application questions, which ask one to think about relationships between ideas such as cause/effect;
- Evaluation questions, which ask one to judge the accuracy of ideas;
- Synthesis questions, which ask one to develop a product by integrating the ideas in the text with ideas of one's own.

Graphic Organizers

Visual representation of how ideas are related to each other. These "pictures"— including Venn diagrams, the T-charts, brainstorming, cluster circles, flow charts, attribute webs, etc.—help students collect information, make interpretations, solve problems, devise plans, and become aware of how they think.

A variety of possible answers should be listed by the teacher, either on large sheets of paper or the chalkboard. Only then should the students be asked to develop their own graphics. Students are encouraged to express their opinions, and to state what they know about a topic. The teacher lists these opinions and "facts" and later, as the students read and research, discovery may be made that some of their ideas are incorrect. These ideas may be crossed out on the sheets or board. Students should be encouraged to elaborate on their answers, justify their opinions, prove their predictions, and relate what they have read to their own lives.

© Novel Units, Inc.   All rights reserved

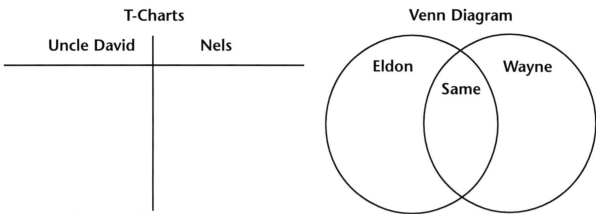

T-Charts

Uncle David	Nels

Venn Diagram

Eldon   Same   Wayne

Cooperative Learning

Learning activities in which groups of two or more students collaborate. There is compelling research evidence that integration of social activities into the learning process—such as small group discussion, group editing, group art projects—often leads to richer, more long-lasting learning.

This book may be read one chapter at a time, using DRTA (Directed Reading Thinking Activity) Method. This technique involves reading a section, predicting what will happen next making good guesses based on what has already occurred in the story. The students continue to read and everyone verifies the prediction.

Before reading, specific vocabulary words will be pointed out. Students may write simple definitions in their own words before reading. After reading, ask students to redefine the words referring to the context or dictionary.

After reading a chapter, brainstorm, "what ifs." What if one or another character wasn't in the story, a character did something different, events followed a different sequence or didn't happen at all, etc. The teacher writes all these "what if" class responses on the board or a large sheet of paper. At the conclusion of the novel, the review of these "what ifs" may be used in writing a different development and/or ending for the novel.

Using Predictions

We all make predictions as we read—little guesses about what will happen next, how the conflict will be resolved, which details given by the author will be important to the plot, which details will help to fill in our sense of a character. Students should be encouraged to predict, to make sensible guesses. As students work on predictions, these discussion questions can be used to guide them: What are some of the ways to predict? What is the process of a sophisticated reader's thinking and predicting? What clues does an author give us to help us in making our predictions? Why are some predictions more likely than others?

A predicting chart is for students to record their predictions. As each subsequent chapter is discussed, you can review and correct previous predictions. This procedure serves to focus on predictions and to review the stories. See page 8 for examples.

© Novel Units, Inc.

All rights reserved

Use the facts and ideas the author gives.

Use your own knowledge.

Use new information that may cause you to change your mind.

Predictions:

_____

_____

_____

_____

Prediction Chart

What characters have we met so far?	What is the conflict in the story?	What are your predictions?	Why did you make those predictions?

© Novel Units, Inc.

All rights reserved

The Course of the Civil War

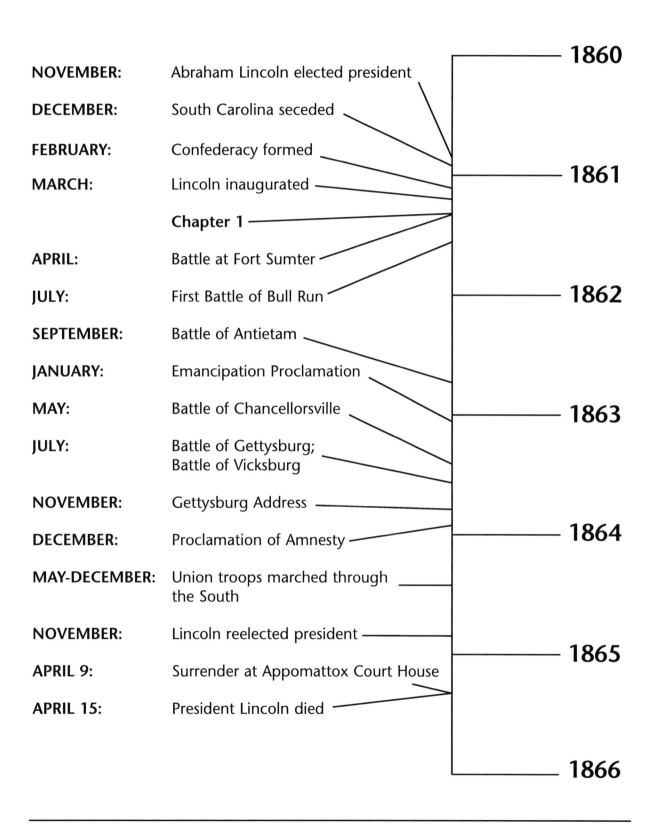

		1860
NOVEMBER:	Abraham Lincoln elected president	
DECEMBER:	South Carolina seceded	
FEBRUARY:	Confederacy formed	
MARCH:	Lincoln inaugurated	**1861**
	Chapter 1	
APRIL:	Battle at Fort Sumter	
JULY:	First Battle of Bull Run	**1862**
SEPTEMBER:	Battle of Antietam	
JANUARY:	Emancipation Proclamation	
MAY:	Battle of Chancellorsville	
JULY:	Battle of Gettysburg; Battle of Vicksburg	**1863**
NOVEMBER:	Gettysburg Address	
DECEMBER:	Proclamation of Amnesty	**1864**
MAY-DECEMBER:	Union troops marched through the South	
NOVEMBER:	Lincoln reelected president	
APRIL 9:	Surrender at Appomattox Court House	**1865**
APRIL 15:	President Lincoln died	
		1866

United States Map

© Novel Units, Inc.

All rights reserved

Anticipation Guide

Directions
Rate each of the following statements before you read the novel. Compare your ratings with a partner's, and discuss why you chose the particular ratings you did. (After you have completed the novel, discuss with your partner whether you would change any of the ratings.)

1 —— 2 —— 3 —— 4 —— 5 —— 6
Agree   **Disagree**
Strongly   **Strongly**

		Before	After
1.	War is exciting.	___	___
2.	Soldiers should follow orders.	___	___
3.	Military deserters are cowards.	___	___
4.	Killing another person is wrong, no matter what.	___	___
5.	Loyalty to your country should come before loyalty to your family.	___	___
6.	The best military leaders have compassion for their troops.	___	___
7.	A true patriot is willing to die for his or her country.	___	___
8.	Few soldiers run from battle.	___	___
9.	It is unpatriotic to criticize military commanders.	___	___
10.	Most soldiers fight because they believe in a cause.	___	___
11.	War is necessary to preserve freedom.	___	___
12.	Soldiers should be proud of their battle injuries.	___	___
13.	"Cowards die many times before their deaths; the valiant taste of death but once." (Shakespeare)	___	___
14.	You should accept your fate.	___	___

© Novel Units, Inc.

All rights reserved

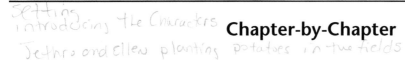
Setting
introducing the Characters
Jethro and Ellen planting potatoes in the fields

Chapter-by-Chapter

Chapter 1   Pages 7-26

Vocabulary

reverberations 8	apathy 11	imminence 12	comeuppance 12
tariffs 14	seceding 14	inclination 15	dissipate 17
intervention 17	waver 18	perplexities 18	amiable 21
coveted 21	rampaging 22	contempt 22	elicited 24
buoyancy 25			

Vocabulary Activity

List the vocabulary words on the board or on a sheet of paper in the form of a table. Pronounce the words. Ask the students to rate their knowledge of each of the words as a group or individually.

Word I Can Define   **I Have Heard**   **I Don't Know**

Discussion Questions and Activities

1. What is a narrator? *(The person who tells a story.)* Who is the narrator of this story? The angle from which the narrator tells the story is called the point of view. The three common points of view are:
    a) First Person: Narration of the story by a character who uses the pronoun "I" in referring to himself.
    b) Omniscient: The narration of a story as though by an all-knowing observer who can see into the minds of all the characters.
    c) Omniscient Third Person: The narrator is all-observing, but limits himself primarily to what one of the characters can know and experience.
        (Across Five Aprils was written in this point of view.)

2. How is Jethro helping his mother when the story begins? *(page 7, planting potatoes)* What kind of a boy is Jethro? Begin an attribute web for him. (See page 32 of this guide.)

3. Where and at what time does their story take place? *(page 7, Southern Illinois, 1861)*

4. Many of the characters in this book speak a Southern country dialect. A dialect is regional variation of language distinguished by pronunciation, grammar, or vocabulary. Keep a list of words that differ from standard English. (e.g., hev = have, fer = for, reckon = suppose)

Why did Wilse G. come to see Creighton family?
What is Calvinism?

5. What does Jethro think about war? *(Page 12, It is exciting and his brothers think the North will win quickly and easily.)* How do Jethro's feelings about war differ from his mother's? *(Jethro's mother fears war and what it can do to her family.)*

6. The author, Irene Hunt, introduces and gives the background of many characters in the first chapter. Make a list of them and their physical and special characteristics. How does Jethro feel about each character?

Chapter 1

Character:	Physical and Special Characteristics	Jethro's Feelings About Character

7. The tragedy of Mary's death and the Burdow family story disturbs Jethro. He questions his father's sense of justice. **Prediction:** What might change his feelings about the Burdows?

8. How does Jethro compare his father to Abraham Lincoln? *(Page 18, He feels anger at his father for not bringing the Burdows to justice and anger toward the President for not getting the war started and over with.)*

9. Who has come from Kentucky for a visit? *(Cousin Wilse Graham from Kentucky comes with news.)* Why is the family so eager for news of the outside world? *(Page 26, They don't get much company and they want to hear news about the possibility of war and other political happenings.)*

Supplementary Activities
1. Locate Kentucky and Southern Illinois on a map of the United States.

2. A story map is an outline that helps you to understand and remember the story better. What do you know about the story after reading only the first chapter?
   - What is the setting?
   - Who is the main character?
   - What is the problem?

   As the story is read, more characters may be added and the setting and the problem may change, so additions may be made. Start the story map on page 33.

3. Chapter Titles: This novel does not have chapter titles. A writer usually uses chapter titles to indicate something that might happen or to create suspense to encourage the reader. After you read a chapter, write what you think would be the best chapter title. The teacher will post all titles and the class will vote for the best. The best chapter titles will be listed on the bulletin board.

Chapter 2   Pages 27-36

Vocabulary

secesh 28	arrogant 29	tremulous 29	abolitionists 30
Mason-Dixon Line 31		tumult 31	vehement 32
industrialism 32	constrained 33	seething 33	

Vocabulary Activity
Students will make predictions about how the author will use the vocabulary, such as setting, characters, problem, action, etc.

Discussion Questions and Activities

1. Why is the Creighton family so troubled about a possible separation of the North and the South? *(Page 28, They are closer in many ways to the people in Missouri and Kentucky than they are to the big city and eastern people of Chicago and New York.)*

2. What does Matthew Creighton mean when he says, "...this separation, Wilse, it won't do. We're a union; separate, we're jest two weakened, puny pieces, each needin' the other"? *(page 29)*

3. What does Wilse say caused the trouble between North and South? *(Page 29, "...half of the country has growed rich, favored by Providence, but still jealous and fearful that the other half is apt to find good fortune too...The high-tariff industrialists would sooner hev the South starve...")*

4. How do John, Bill and Cousin Wilse differ on their views of slavery? *(Pages 29-31, John—It is wrong for one man owning body and soul of another; Page 30, Wilse— There's always been slavery from the beginning of history; Bill—He hates slavery but the trouble over slavery grows because of the North's greed.)*

5. Why do you think Mrs. Creighton doesn't want anyone to talk about war?

Prediction
Bill and John have different opinions about the war. Do you think one will change his mind? Who? Why?

river states
Missouri
Kentucky

Lyle Graham coming
Creightons have supper with Wilse & Graham
and talk about slavery and the war.

S. Illinois closer Missouri and Kentucky

© Novel Units, Inc.   All rights reserved

Bill has a fight w/ brother John over the war.
Bill leaves S. Ill. for Kentucky to fight for the South
He doesn't believe either
He believes both sides are wrong (or to blame) but feels stronger for the South ?

Supplementary Activities

1. Literary Analysis: Conflict is the struggle between two or more forces. There are external conflicts—character struggle against an outside force such as nature, society or another person and internal conflict where the struggle takes place within a characters own mind. There are three main types of conflict:
   a) Person-against-person
   b) Person-against-nature/society
   c) Person-against-self
   What kinds of conflict are found in this chapter? Begin the Nature of Conflict Chart on page 34.

2. Research arguments for and against slavery.

3. Research arguments for and against tariffs.

Jeth talks about his love for Walnut Hill and his imag. playmates.

Chapter 3

The war is coming closer to Illinois with Wilson's Creek

Pages 37-46

Vocabulary

prestige 37	oratory 37	tedium 37	fiasco 38
chafed 38	emancipator 39	nullification 41	blithely 42
tumult 42	wastrel 42	silhouetted 44	perplexity 44

Vocabulary Activity

The students will develop word maps. They will use color to distinguish antonyms, synonyms, etc. This activity may be done in cooperative groups.

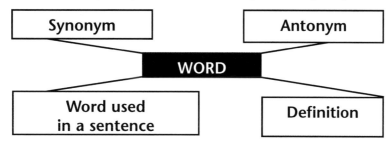

Discussion Questions and Activities

1. How do the people turn the preparation for war into one long party? *(Page 37, They have big picnics, brass bands and speakers. Pretty girls plan ways to collect money for the troops.)*

2. Who wins the Battle of Bull Run? *(Page 38, Union troops are turned back.)*

3. How do the Battles of Bull Run and Ball's Bluff change the spirit of the times? *(Page 38, The people begin to realize that war means killing of young men and that the war will not easily be won by the North.)*

© Novel Units, Inc.   All rights reserved

4. Literary Analysis: Tone is the author's emotional attitude as presented in the story. The author shares his characters' moods and the moods are reflected in the environment and in the author's choice of details in presenting the facts. How does Jethro's nightmare and his talk with Bill set the tone for the novel? *(Pages 40-41, Jethro is upset and scared because of the talk about war. Bill's talk with him set an atmosphere for how terrible war is.)* *full of fire* *alive*

5. Explain Bill's words, "...this war has been fanned by hate till it's a blaze now; and a blaze kin destroy him that makes it and him that the fire was set to hurt." *(page 41)* *hate* *Nobody wins a war* *There shouldn't have been a war.*

6. Why do Bill and John have a fight? *(Pages 44-46, Bill's leaving home to fight for the South sparks the fight. Bill believes fighting for the North is fighting for factory owners and big money rather than for the farmer.)*

Prediction
Do you think Bill's decision to fight for the South will change Jethro's feelings for him? How might they change?

Supplementary Activities
1. **Research:** How could work in the factories be compared to slavery? (page 41) Complete the following chart.

	Slavery	Factory Work in 1830	Factory Work Today
Length of Workday		13 hours	8 hours or less
Length of Workweek		6 or 7 days	5 days
Overtime Pay		Almost none	At least 1-1/2 times normal pay
Paid Vacations		Almost none	2-4 weeks per year
Paid Holidays		Almost none	10 per year
Hospital Insurance		None	Provided by many employers

2. **Writing:** Assume the role of Jethro. After each chapter, jot down an entry about what has happened and how you feel about it in your "diary."

Why is Bill living in the South?
Why is John living in the South and fighting for the North?
Are Tom and Ed going to fight in the war and for the North/South?

All rights reserved

Vocabulary

capitulation 48	admonitions 52	tyrannical 55	allusion 55
rebuke 59	pompous 61	constriction 61	maneuvering 62
distortions 62	skepticism 63		

Vocabulary Activity

Place the words for the day in categories. For example:

Descriptive   **Feelings**   **Actions**   **Things**   **People**

Discussion Questions and Activities

1. What is the first real victory for the North? *(page 47, the fall of Fort Henry in Tennessee)*

2. Literary Analysis—Characterization: The author may present his characters directly or indirectly. In direct presentation he tells us straight out what a character is like or has someone else in the story tell us what he/she is like.

   In indirect presentation, the author shows us the character in action; we infer what he is like from what he thinks or says or does.

   To be convincing, characterization must also observe three other principles—first, characters must be consistent in their behavior. They must not behave one way on one occasion and a different way on another unless there is a sufficient reason for change. Second, characters must be clearly motivated in whatever they do, especially when there is any change in behavior. Third, characters must be plausible or lifelike.

   Change in character:
   • Must be within the possibilities of character who makes it;
   • Must be sufficiently motivated by circumstances in which a character finds himself;
   • Must be allowed sufficient time for change to believably take place.

3. How is Jethro changing in this chapter? How are his feelings for his family changing?

4. What things do we know about Mrs. Creighton? *(She had 12 children; she worked hard in the fields as well as cooking, cleaning, and working for her family; she was from Kentucky; she couldn't read but she respected education; and she worried about all her children.)* Begin an attribute web for Mrs. Creighton.

© Novel Units, Inc.

All rights reserved

5. Why do you think Mrs. Creighton sent Jethro to visit Shad? *(pages 50-51, So the grown-ups could talk, to give Jethro some happy company, and to share Tom's letter with Shad.)*

6. How is Shad like a member of the family? *(He is the schoolmaster in love with Jethro's sister; Ellen has treated him as part of the family since nursing him back to health when he had typhoid fever.)*

7. How do Ma and Pa differ on the subject of Jenny's marrying Shad? *(Page 55, Ma approves but Pa thinks Jenny is too young.)*

8. Shad says Mr. Creighton is being tyrannical about Jenny. Can you present Matthew Creighton's reasons for Jenny not marrying Shad before the war is over? *(page 55)*

9. Jethro feels a twinge of loyalty for his father. If you had been Jethro, what would you have said to Shad? *(page 55)*

10. What do you know about Shad? Begin an attribute web for him.

11. Why do people, not only in the South, criticize Abraham Lincoln? *(Page 60, Abolitionists hate him; people blame Lincoln for the generals' mistakes; and make fun of his grammar, his appearance and family.)*

Supplementary Activity
Literary Analysis: Authors sometimes use figurative language to make descriptions more vivid for readers. **Similes** are comparisons using the words "like" or "as." A **metaphor** is a comparison between two things, without the words "like" or "as." **Personification** is giving human characteristics to an animal or an object. Make a list of figurative language used in this novel.

Vocabulary

appalled 65	passel 67	exhilarated 68	inevitably 69
precariously 72	decisive 74	assurance 74	dissipated 76
Copperhead 76	inconspicuous 77	astute 79	caustically 79
terrain 84	revulsion 84	floundered 84	resonance 85
plaintive 87			

Vocabulary Activity

Take the vocabulary words for several chapters. Play a 20 questions-type game (pairs, groups, or whole class). One student, or the teacher, selects a word for the class or group to identify by asking up to 20 questions (or 10 questions) about that word which may be answered by "yes," "no," or "sometimes."

Discussion Questions and Activities

1. How has Nancy begun to change since John left? *(Pages 66-67, She has grown more talkative, inviting Jethro to play more with her boys.)*

2. Why do you think ten-year-old Jethro is given the job of driving to town? *(Page 68, No men are left to do the farm work. It will not be easy for Jethro to drive the team but that will be easier than the farm jobs.)*

3. What trouble does Jethro run into in town? *(Page 75, Guy Wortman starts harassing him, calling Bill a "rebel" and a "Copperhead.")*

4. What do we know about Guy Wortman, the man who picked on Jethro? *(Pages 75-76 and 81, He likes to drum up mob violence, hasn't joined the army, and loafs around the store and drinks.)*

5. How does Jethro handle Wortman? *(Pages 75-76, He speaks up for Bill and his father.)*

6. What did you learn about an 1860's town? *(mud streets, box-like cabins, wooden sidewalks, town built around a square, jail without doors, not many stores)*

7. How do people show kindness to Jethro? *(Pages 77-78, Free candy, Ross Milton gives him a book on usage and speech and dinner in a restaurant.)*

8. Why does Burdow wait for Jethro on the road? *(Pages 85-86, Burdow knows that Jethro could be ambushed and wants to protect him.)*

Prediction
Will the Burdows try to make up to the Creightons?

Supplementary Activities
1. **Art**
   Draw a picture of the town as Jethro saw it.
2. **Drama**
   What could Jethro and Burdow have said on the ride?
3. **Research**
   Conscription/The Draft was used during the Civil War as volunteer enlistment decreased. The first Southern draft law was passed in April, 1862 and made all able-bodied white men from ages 18 through 35 liable for three years' service. By February 1864, the limits had been changed to 17 and 50. The Northern program, begun in March 1863, drafted men from ages 20 through 45 for three years. Exceptions to the draft were made in the North and South. Both sides allowed a draftee to pay a substitute to serve for him. In addition, a draftee in the North could pay the government $300 to avoid military service. The system seemed unfair, and many soldiers complained that they were involved in "a rich man's war and a poor man's fight." On the whole, both armies had a fair representation of soldiers from the various social groups of their regions. The draft worked poorly and was extremely unpopular in many areas of both North and South. In some isolated hill country of the South, it could not be enforced. However, the Northern and Southern draft succeeded in its main purpose, which was to stimulate volunteering. (Source: *The World Book Encyclopedia*, 1991)

Chapter 6 **Pages 90-107**

Vocabulary
quagmire 92 ultimatum 97 tranquil 98 dissipated 99
raucous 104 gullibility 106 chagrin 106 culprit 107
malice 107

Vocabulary Activity
For each of the vocabulary words write a sentence that makes sense. Omit the vocabulary word. Make an answer key on the back of the paper. Share your sentences with a classmate.

Discussion Questions and Activities
1. What happens to Matt Creighton? *(Page 91, He has a heart attack or stroke.)* How do you think this will affect Jethro?

2. How does the continuing war affect the Creightons? *(Prices for things they buy are high; they worry about their boys; and some people threaten the Creightons because Bill is fighting for the South.)*

3. Who burns down the Creightons' barn and pours oil in their well? Why do they do this? *(pages 104-106, drunken men who call the Creightons Copperheads)*

4. How do most of the Creightons' neighbors react when they learn about how the family has been threatened? *(Pages 105-107, They are supportive.)*

5. What were the effects of war on people in the United States? Brainstorm. Record student responses on a large sheet of paper. Research Project: Complete a chart like the one below.

Effects of the Civil War on the United States	
Good Effects	**Bad Effects**
High employment	Not enough people to do farm and factory work
Slaves freed	Result—scarcity of many things—high prices
	Divided families
	Many people killed
	Crops, buildings and cities destroyed
	Government torn apart

Vocabulary

integrity 111   plaudits 111   tenacious 115   inept 116

Vocabulary Activity

List the vocabulary words for the day on large sheets of paper. Leave space for students to:

    a) illustrate the meaning next to each word;
    b) list a memory device to remember the word;
    c) show how to pronounce the word by using dictionary symbols.

Discussion Questions and Activities

1. How does news of Tom's death reach the Creightons? *(Page 109, Dan Lawrence, a neighbor, had been with Tom when he was killed.)*

2. The Creightons had lost several of their children in accidents, illness and war. How do they handle the news of this death?

3. What is the purpose of Ross Milton's open letter in the newspaper? *(pages 110-111, to put an end to the harassment of the Creightons by pointing out that Tom has died fighting for the Union)*

4. How did you feel when you read the open letter in Ross Milton's paper?

5. How does Wortman become the laughing stock of the county? *(Pages 115-116, Sam Gardiner, proprietor of the general store, pretends that he is away from the store; when Wortman and the ruffians strike, he blasts Wortman in the backside with buckshot.)* How else could he have stopped Wortman?

6. How does the war progress in the summer of 1862? *(Pages 117-118, Nothing seems to be working for the North. The South seems to have better generals.)*

7. In which Northern generals are Jethro and others beginning to lose faith? Why? *(Pages 117-118, Halleck and McClellan boast ineffectually; Pope and Sheridan bluster; and Grant drinks.)*

Supplementary Activities

1. Create an illustrated time line on which you mark the key events of the story.
2. Analyze the values of the main characters: Jethro, Shad, Bill, Tom, and Ross Milton.

© Novel Units, Inc.   All rights reserved

Vocabulary

    plummeted 125   obscurity 125   dissuaded 126

Vocabulary Activity

In cooperative groups make bingo cards using the vocabulary words from all the chapters completed. The cards may be added to as the book is read. The caller of the game may use the vocabulary word or the word definitions.

Discussion Questions and Activities

1. How much time has passed since the story started? *(one and a half years)* How old is Jethro now? *(10 years old)* How has Jethro changed?

2. Why is it so important for the Union to win the piece of the Mississippi River between Baton Rouge and Vicksburg from the Confederates? *(page 119, doing so will cut the Confederacy in half)*

3. Why does Dave Burdow send a load of logs with Ross Milton? *(Page 121, He wants to show he is sorry for all the tragedies of the Creightons and he knows Ross Milton will deliver the logs and the right message.)*

4. Why does Jethro have to force himself to be quiet as he listens to discussion of the war? *(Pages 123-124, He doesn't agree with things the men say but he knows that a boy has no right to contradict a man's opinion.)*

5. How does the Battle of Antietam affect Shad? *(Page 124, He is very disturbed to see death and suffering.)*

6. What does Shad think of General McClellan? *(Pages 125, He doesn't dislike him, but feels that McClellan needs to be less fearful of making decisions, must show more brutal tenacity.)*

7. Why are there so many deserters? *(Page 127, The men are disillusioned; there is no end to the war in sight.)*

Supplementary Activity

Develop a Cause and Effect Chart. (See page 35 of this guide.)

© Novel Units, Inc.   All rights reserved

Vocabulary

deserters 128	forays 128	gangrenous 129	antagonized 133
tethered 133	credence 135	audible 136	interminable 144
impudent 144	intrude 146	forfeiture 147	

Vocabulary Activity

Put the vocabulary words in alphabetical order. Arrange the words into sets of two words. Since there are 11 words, there should be five sets of two words each with one word left over. Use each set of two words in the same sentence.

Discussion Questions and Activities

1. How could men avoid the Civil War draft? *(Page 129, Pay a $300 fee and find a substitute to take his place.)* Do you think this was fair? Why or why not?

2. What is going on at Point Prospect campground? *(Pages 128-129, Deserters gather down there.)* Why don't the Federal Registrars go there to get the deserters? *(They are afraid and don't want to be shot.)*

3. Why do the representatives of the Federal Registrars come to the Creightons' house? *(Page 130, They are looking for Ebenezer Carron who had lived with the Creightons since he was 10 years old.)*

4. Why do the Federal Registrars make fun of Jethro's speech? *(Page 132, They are city men probably from up North. They laugh about Jethro's southern Illinois drawl and his backwoods diction.)*

5. How does Eb contact Jethro? What does Eb want from Jethro? *(Pages 133-136, Eb gives a wild turkey call from the woods near where Jethro is plowing; he says he wants to hear about the family.)*

6. Why did Eb desert the army? What other choices did he have? *(Pages 135-138, The armies had a battle and Eb had to bury dead soldiers. He just left and he did not have too many choices because deserter camps were awful.)*

7. Do you think Jethro is right in not telling his family about Eb? Why or why not?

8. Why does Jethro write a letter to President Lincoln? Why is this a good solution to his problem and to Eb's problem? *(pages 142-144)*

9. How do you think Jethro's family will react to the letter from the President? How do you think they will treat Eb? What will they say? *(pages 146-147)*

© Novel Units, Inc.   All rights reserved

Prediction
What do you think will become of Eb now?

Supplementary Activities
1. Research deserters in the Civil War.
2. Role Play/Interview: A panel of five students sits facing the class, which has prepared a list of questions to ask the characters in the story. Each panel member wears something and/or carries a simple prop which characterizes the role that person is assuming.

Chapter 10   Pages 148-159

Vocabulary

arrogant 148	contemptuous 148	onslaught 148	besieged 150
discredited 151	verified 151	incoherent 152	pandemonium 152

Vocabulary Activity
Find the base or root word of each vocabulary word. In cooperative groups make word maps using the models on page 31.

Discussion Questions and Activities
1. Who wins the Battle of Chancellorsville? Which of the characters in the story is there? *(Page 148, The Confederates; Shad is there.)*

2. How is Eb treated by the other soldiers when he returns to the war? How does he feel about being back? *(Page 150, Some of the soldiers criticize him, but he accepts that he must "take it" and is relieved to be back, although the heat, dirt, and work are hard.)*

3. What is the capital of the Confederacy? Why might the Confederacy deliberately allow it to be taken by Union troops? *(page 151, Richmond; in exchange for taking Washington, D.C.)*

4. Who wins the Battle of Gettysburg? How long is it? *(page 152, Union victory; three bloody days)*

5. Which character is seriously wounded at Gettysburg? Why is he in Washington? *(Page 153, Shad; He is brought from Gettysburg to Washington, D.C. where his aunt lives.)*

6. Why does Matt Creighton allow Jenny to go to Washington to see Shad? *(Page 154, Ross Milton convinces him it is the thing to do. It might help save Shad's life.)*

© Novel Units, Inc.   All rights reserved

7. Do you think Jenny and her parents made the right decision for her to marry at 16? Why or why not? How was marriage at 16 in 1863 different from today?

8. Jethro uses Ross Milton's usage book to write his letter but the letter isn't perfect. How would you improve it? *(page 159)*

Prediction
Do you think that Shad, Eb, and John will return from the war or die of injuries or in battle?

Supplementary Activities
1. **Art**
   Have students choose a part of the story which they believe should be illustrated.

2. **Drama**
   Divide the class into groups of three. Each person in the group will assume the role of a character in the novel. Each person will retell the story (or an incident from a chapter) from his/her point of view. The students will imitate the character with voice and gestures.

Chapter 11   Pages 160-173

Vocabulary

prominence 161	provender 162	vindictiveness 165	amnesty 165
deluded 165	relegated 165	invective 166	

Vocabulary Activity
Place the vocabulary words in the following possible categories.

Describes an emotion	Animals can taste it	Is a verb
Deserters desire this	You can see it	Is a noun
Is an adjective	You can taste it	You can smell it
You can touch it		

Discussion Questions and Activities

1. What does Abraham Lincoln's proclamation of amnesty mean? *(Page 165, "...pardon and full rights to any individual Confederate who would swear to protect the Constitution and the Union of the states, to abide by the government's pronouncements against slavery.")*

2. Why is the North against the proclamation of amnesty? Why is the South against it? What does Lincoln try to do? *(Page 165, The North considers that Lincoln's proclamation of amnesty "was little better than treason...and many people began to consider it high patriotism to talk of the coming wholesale execution of rebels." "In the South the Confederate Congress cried out that if the Washington government called for restoration of the Union it was merely setting a cruel trap for the deluded...that it would mean personal and public degradation and ruin.")*

3. How do Jethro and Matt Creighton feel about Lincoln? *(Page 165, They respect and love him.)*

4. Of what political party is President Lincoln a member? *(page 167, Republican)*

5. For which presidential candidate do most of the soldiers vote? *(page 170, Lincoln)* Which Northern states do not give most of the vote to Lincoln? *(Pages 170-171, Kentucky, Delaware, and New Jersey do not give their vote for Lincoln.)*

6. How do the Creightons learn that Bill is still alive? *(Page 173, John writes that he has found Bill among the Rebel prisoners of war.)*

7. Explain: "Bill wants that I shood tell you this—he was not at Pittsburg Landing. That bullet was not fired by him..." *(Page 173, Bill wants his mother to know that he did not kill his brother Tom.)*

Prediction
What do you think will happen to Bill and John? What were the prisoner of war camps like? Why did so many prisoners die?

Vocabulary

tenacity 176	degradation 179	imminence 179	bigots 180
ratified 180	pawns 180	exploiters 180	serenity 183

Vocabulary Activity

Decide what other prefixes and suffixes may be added to vocabulary words and note how these change the word meanings.

Discussion Questions and Activities

1. What happens on Sherman's march through Georgia? Why are some people critical of the "picnic" the Union soldiers have along the way? What is your opinion of the way they act? *(Pages 175-177, Sherman's army sacks, loots, and burns; many feel that the pillaging is wrong and will make it even harder for the North and South to heal their wounds.)*

2. What state—"where secesh was hatched"—is plundered after Georgia? *(page 176, South Carolina)*

3. Why are Jethro's parents worried about him? *(Page 178, He has grown more reserved and serious. Jethro's parents worry that they will lose him as they lost Bill.)*

4. How does Ross Milton "rip up his [Jethro's] dream of peace"? *(Page 179, He points out how long and hard the road to healing will be.)*

5. What is the 13th amendment? *(page 180, abolition of slavery)*

6. When is peace declared? Where? How long has the war lasted? *(Page 181, Terms of peace are signed at Appomattox Court House, Virginia; April, 1865; 4 years.)*

7. What tragedy happens to make that "fifth April...a time of grief and desolation"? *(Page 183, Lincoln is assassinated.)*

8. How do Jethro's feelings about war change during the book? Why do you think they change?

9. What are Shad's plans for himself and for Jethro? How does Shad try to convince Jethro that it is all right to give up his responsibilities on the farm? Do you think Jethro will be convinced? *(Pages 187-188, Shad wants to go back to college and to have Jethro come to live with him and Jenny while Jethro continues his studies; Shad points out that Eb and John can help on the farm and that John wants Jethro to get an education so Jethro can help his boys get one.)*

© Novel Units, Inc.   All rights reserved

Post-reading Questions and Activities

1. Summarize the story using the story diagram below. What purpose is there in a story diagram? How would using a story map help an author?

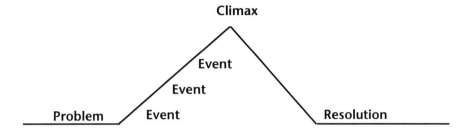

2. Characterization: Characters are developed by what they say, think, and do and by how others in the novel react to them. Review the attribute webs. Which characters in this novel provided wisdom and perspective? Which character in the story is most like you? Do you find the characters in the book "real"? How did the characters change during the story? Review character change. How would you explain the changes in characters in this novel?

3. Theme is the novel's central idea. What is the author's message? Why do you think the author wrote this story? What do you think is the most important thing to remember about this story? Support your ideas for the theme or themes by examples from the novel. Is the central theme of this story presented directly or indirectly?

4. Summarize the story by making a collage of key characters, pictures or symbols, and important words.

5. How important was the setting to the story? Could the story have taken place in another time or place? (WWII, Vietnam War) If so, what would change?

6. Which parts of this story were most vivid and interesting to you? Which parts made you laugh? Did any parts make you cry?

© Novel Units, Inc.   All rights reserved

7. Use the diagram below with a partner or small group to free-associate thoughts about the novel after you have finished it. Jot down your thoughts in a similar format on a large piece of paper.

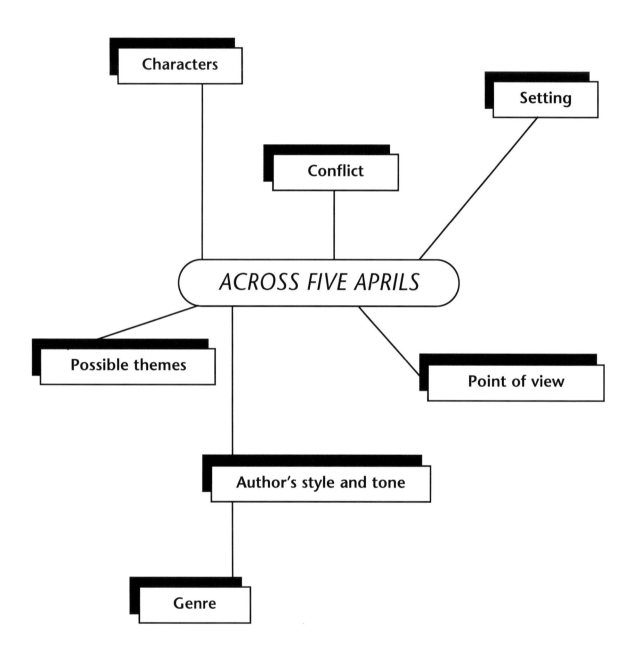

© Novel Units, Inc.　　　　　　　　　　　　　　　　All rights reserved

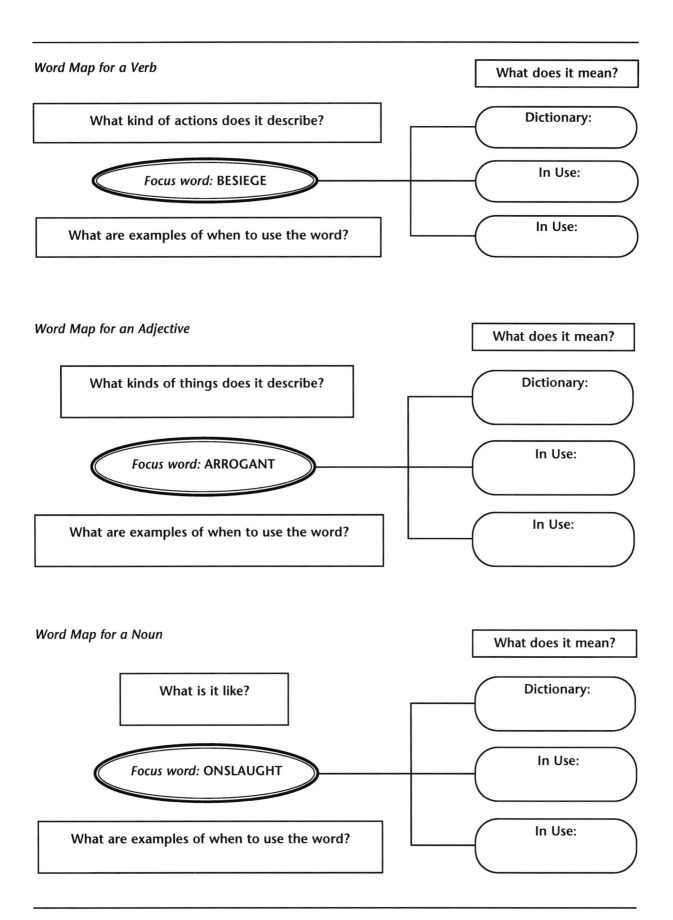

Word Map for a Verb

What does it mean?

What kind of actions does it describe?

Focus word: BESIEGE

Dictionary:

In Use:

In Use:

What are examples of when to use the word?

Word Map for an Adjective

What does it mean?

What kinds of things does it describe?

Focus word: ARROGANT

Dictionary:

In Use:

In Use:

What are examples of when to use the word?

Word Map for a Noun

What does it mean?

What is it like?

Focus word: ONSLAUGHT

Dictionary:

In Use:

In Use:

What are examples of when to use the word?

© Novel Units, Inc.

All rights reserved

Attribute Web

The attribute web below is designed to help you gather clues the author provides about what a character is like. Fill in the blanks with words and phrases which tell how the character acts and looks, as well as what the character says and what others say about him or her.

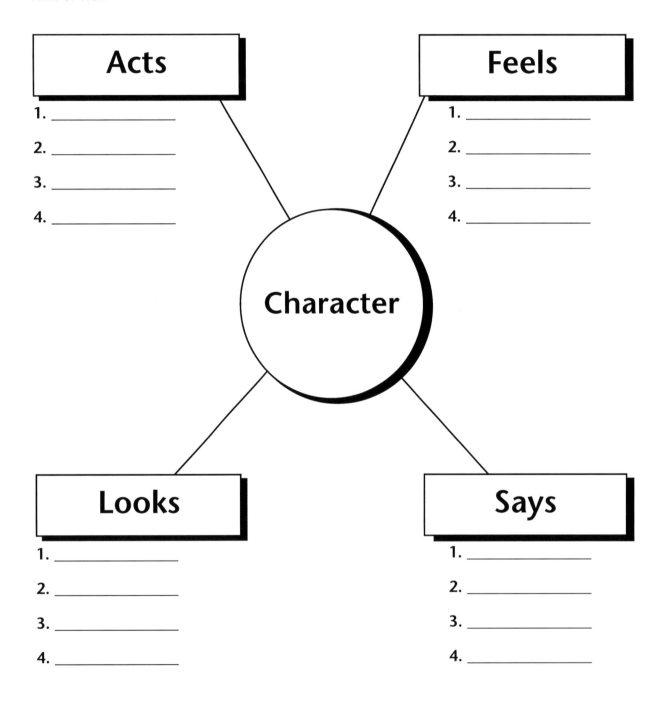

© Novel Units, Inc.

All rights reserved

Story Map

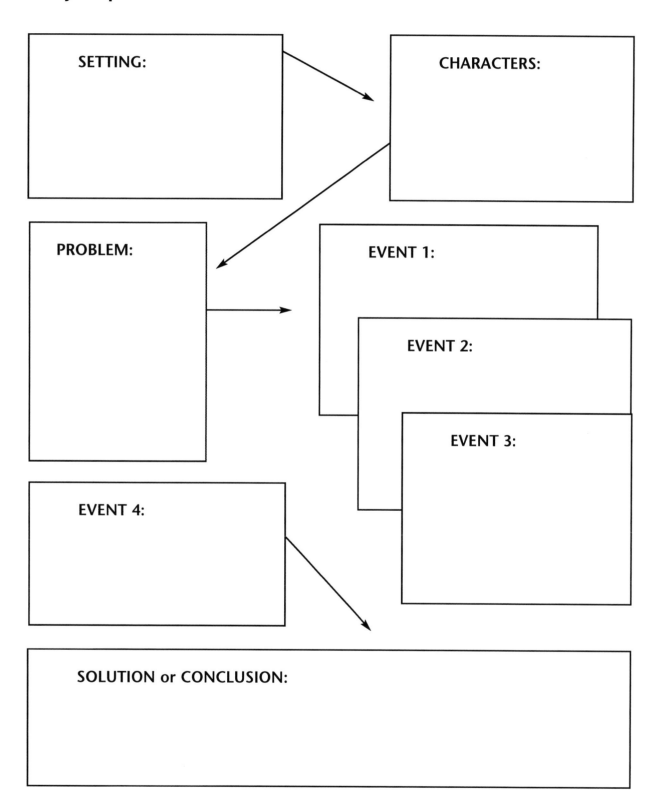

SETTING:

CHARACTERS:

PROBLEM:

EVENT 1:

EVENT 2:

EVENT 3:

EVENT 4:

SOLUTION or CONCLUSION:

© Novel Units, Inc.

33

All rights reserved

The Nature of Conflict

As is true in real life, the characters in novels face many conflicts. When two people or forces struggle over the same thing, conflict occurs. The excitement in novels develops from the use of the three main types of conflict: (1) person against person; (2) person against nature or society; and (3) person against himself or herself.

Below list some of the conflicts from the novel. In the space provided, briefly describe the conflict and indicate which type of conflict is involved, writing "PP" for person vs. person, "PN" for person vs. nature or society, and "PS" for person vs. self. Then choose three of the conflicts and describe how each was resolved.

Conflict	Description	Type

Conflict #1 resolution:

_____

Conflict #2 resolution:

_____

Conflict #3 resolution:

_____

© Novel Units, Inc.   All rights reserved

Cause/Effect Chart

Directions
When examining the reason for events in a story, we often find that:
  a) one cause has several results, or
  b) several causes lead to the same result.

1. Think about the various effects the Civil War has on the Creighton family.

How does the Civil War affect the Creighton family?

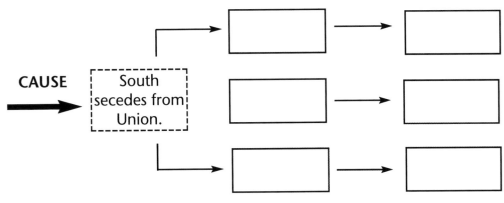

2. Think about why the Creightons act as they do. Organize some of these reasons (causes) within the map below.

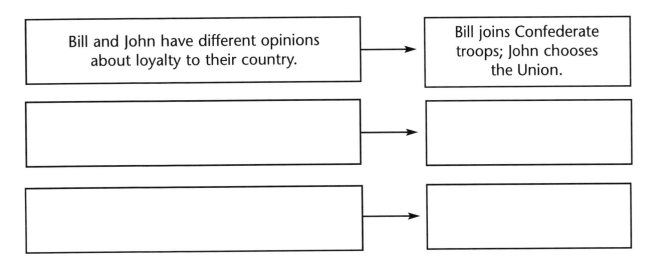

All rights reserved

Assessment for *Across Five Aprils*

Assessment is an ongoing process, more than a quiz at the end of the book. Points may be added to show the level of achievement. When an item is completed, the teacher and the student check it.

Name _____ Date _____

Student   **Teacher**

_____   _____   1. Complete the story map (page 33) or make one of your own.

_____   _____   2. Give yourself one point for each vocabulary activity completed successfully.

_____   _____   3. Write chapter titles that indicate something that might happen or to create suspense to encourage the reader.

_____   _____   4. Complete one of the suggested research projects: arguments for or against slavery, for or against tariffs, comparison of slavery and factory work, conscription in the Civil War, deserters in the Civil War. Make a presentation using graphic organizers.

_____   _____   5. Make an attribute web for one of the characters in the novel.

_____   _____   6. Create a collage to represent important ideas of the book.

_____   _____   7. Complete the Conflict Chart on page 34.

_____   _____   8. Create an illustrated time line on which you mark the key events of the story.

_____   _____   9. Change three things in this novel and explain to a classmate how the changes would make a difference.

_____   _____   10. What did you learn about the Civil War that you did not know before reading this novel? Write three paragraphs to share with classmates and your parents.

All rights reserved